Australian Geographic
THE KIMBERLEY

By Katrina O'Brien

WOODSLANE PRESS

Woodslane Press Pty Ltd
10 Apollo Street
Warriewood, NSW 2102
Email: info@woodslane.com.au
Tel: 02 8445 2300 Website: www.woodslane.com.au

First published in Australia in 2018 by Woodslane Press in association with Australian Geographic
© 2018 Woodslane Press, photographs © Australian Geographic and others
(see acknowledgements on page 62)

A catalogue record for this book is available from the National Library of Australia

MIX
Paper from responsible sources
FSC® C151165

Printed in China by Asia Pacific Offset
Cover image: Purnululu National Park by Nick Rains © Australian Geographic
Book design by: Christine Schiedel

CONTENTS

THE KIMBERLEY

Ihe Kimberley is part of Australia's tropical north with a summer monsoon that throws a green cloak over the grassy plains and scrub-covered ranges, and turns the rivers into powerful torrents. During the dry season the rivers shrink to a series of pools, waterfalls slow to a trickle and the heat and humidity drop to a comfortable warmth that people and creatures flock north to enjoy. There are only three major roads in the Kimberley and just one of them is sealed – the Great Northern Highway from Broome to Kununurra. Broome is a sophisticated coastal resort of entirely unique character, while Kununurra on the eastern edge of the region is surrounded by beautiful Kimberley range country and fertile land fed by the Ord River.

The Gibb River Road connects these towns and provides access to the region's most beautiful gorges in cattle country but this is a challenging route. Halfway along this road, along an even rougher track, the Kalumbaru Road, heads north to the coast, with a side track to the Mitchell Plateau. There are many places so remote that you can only see them by boat, plane or 4WD, such as the Dampier Peninsula, Buccaneer Archipelago and the Bungle Bungle Range in Purnululu National Park. There's no doubt that it takes commitment to travel in the Kimberley but it will reward you with a sense of adventure, achievement and the feeling that nothing matters but this moment that you're alive in one of the world's oldest living landscapes.

Above: Fossilised *Megalosauropus broomensis* dinosaur tracks thought to be 130 million years old can be seen at very low spring tides at Gant-heaume Point, Broome. Even more excitingly, just to the north of Broome, in the James Price Point area, scientists discovered the world's biggest dinosaur tracks, belonging to a sauropod with 1.7 m long feet. There are about 21 different kinds of dinosaur prints in the area.

Left: Frill-necked lizard at rest. These common Kimberley lizards only flare their frill when they feel threatened. They spend most of their time in trees and eat insects, spiders and smaller lizards.

■ Left: The Kimberley's ancient geology is on display wherever you turn. The changing movements of the seas in which these rocks were formed can be seen in the cross-bedding patterns of this tower in Mirima National Park near Kununurra.

THE KIMBERLEY

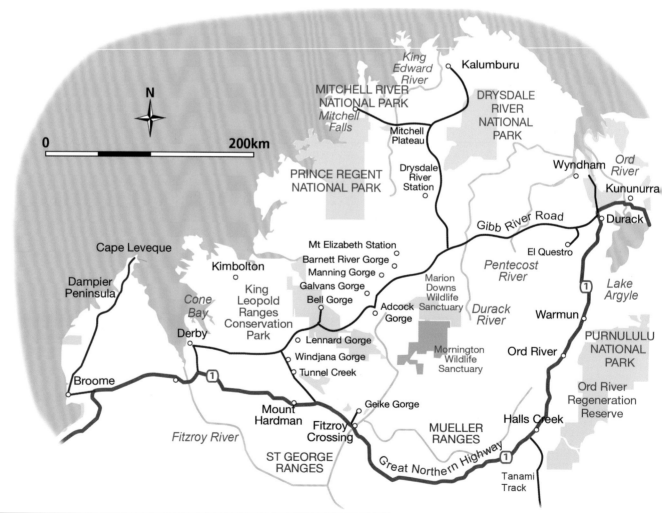

N

0   200km

King Edward River

Kalumburu

MITCHELL RIVER NATIONAL PARK

Mitchell Falls

Mitchell Plateau

DRYSDALE RIVER NATIONAL PARK

Wyndham

Ord River

Kununurra

Drysdale River Station

PRINCE REGENT NATIONAL PARK

Gibb River Road

Durack

El Questro

Cape Leveque

Mt Elizabeth Station

Barnett River Gorge

Manning Gorge

Pentecost River

Lake Argyle

Dampier Peninsula

Kimbolton

Cone Bay

King Leopold Ranges Conservation Park

Galvans Gorge

Bell Gorge

Marion Downs Wildlife Sanctuary

Durack River

Warmun

PURNULULU NATIONAL PARK

Adcock Gorge

Derby

Lennard Gorge

Mornington Wildlife Sanctuary

Ord River

Ord River Regeneration Reserve

Windjana Gorge

Broome

Tunnel Creek

Geike Gorge

Halls Creek

Mount Hardman

Fitzroy Crossing

MUELLER RANGES

Fitzroy River

Great Northern Highway

ST GEORGE RANGES

Tanami Track

■ Above: The 100-metre twin waterfalls of King George Falls dwarf a cruise boat floating below. These falls, 250 km north west of Kununurra, are only accessible by boat or scenic flight and are most impressive in April and May.

GEOLOGY

Australia is an ancient land and in the Kimberley its bones are laid bare. This region is the oldest in the country, with rocks that are virtually all more than 350 million years old. What makes the Kimberley particularly special is that there has been so little geological activity since the rocks were formed. The last period of mountain building was 1700 million years ago. In the King Leopold and Halls Creek orogens (eroded remnants of ancient mountain belts) there is evidence of the characteristic faulting and folding which occurs during the formation of mountain ranges. Yet this rock has had an unimaginably long time to erode. Around 350 million years ago much of the Kimberley's lowland was under water. Windjana and Geike Gorges offer a rich snapshot back to this time, displaying some of the best fossil reefs in the world. These limestone ranges were built by cyanobacteria and other carbonate-secreting organisms. The rainwater dissolving the limestone has formed cave systems, a good example of which is seen at Tunnel Creek. The sandstone of the Carr Boyd and Cockburn ranges has been strongly compacted and cemented - collapsing in slabs along vertical fractures rather than the grain by grain erosion of the Bungle Bungle range. The result is the rugged cliffs beneath a flat-topped plateau that dominate the view when crossing the Pentecost River.

Above: Fossilised shoreline ripples in ancient Kimberley sandstone.

Left: Tunnel Creek in the Napier Range is part of the 350 million year old Devonian Reef system that includes Windjana Gorge 35 km to the north west. You can walk and wade through the 750 m-long tunnel. Take a torch to look out for bats and wear sturdy sandals.

CLIMATE

When planning a visit to the Kimberley it's essential to choose the right time of year. It's a tropical monsoon climate which means there are essentially two seasons, the Dry and the Wet. About 90% of the region's annual rainfall – that's about 1300 mm in the north west and 500 mm in the south east – falls during the Wet. The Dry season from May to October is perfect for travelling, with sunny skies and stable warm weather. The Wet brings very hot steamy days with dramatic afternoon storms and heavy rains. Many locals say the Wet is their favourite time of year but for visitors it can be a difficult time to travel, roads are often closed, many resorts shut down for the season, and it's not unusual for there to be one or two cyclones each season. Aboriginal groups in the Kimberley recognise four to six seasons, defined by regular changes in wind, rain, temperature, and clouds, as well as the movements of animals and flowering of plants.

■ Storm clouds gathering over Manning Gorge, on the Gibb River Road, at sunset.

SUMMER
■ (December – March)
This is the wet season when temperatures are about 25-37°C and the humidity is relentless. Rainfall is unpredictable but heavy when it comes, with the risk of flooding. The land blooms with a profusion of grass, flowers and wildlife.

AUTUMN
■ (April – May)
Rainfall should have come to end by April but it's still very hot (20-35°C) and humid. Locals will be watching rivers and roads to see if waters have dropped low enough to make them navigable. Once the roads are open, May (18-33°C) is a superb time to see thundering waterfalls.

WINTER
■ (June – August)
Endless sunny days with temperatures from 15-30 °C, though inland country like Purnululu National Park can get much colder than that overnight. This is peak tourist season and a wonderful time to be in the Kimberley. August days will start to feel hotter and waterfalls may have disappeared.

SPRING
■ (September – November)
September and October will see temperatures from about 21-37°C. It's the end of the season and most visitors have left by now and the land will be looking very dry, though you might get the odd afternoon shower. By November many operators have shut up shop because it's the hottest month of the year, stormy and humid, from 25°C overnight to highs of 39-40°C.

PEOPLE

The Kimberley is most often described as 'remote' and this north western corner of Australia is the furthest region from the south eastern coastline where most Australians live. Yet its proximity to India and Asia meant that there had been a succession of visitors for hundreds of years before Captain Cook set foot in Botany Bay in 1770. Macassans from the Indonesian island of Sulawesi had been coming since around 1500 to harvest trepang (sea slug). In the early seventeenth century Dutch mariners, transporting goods to Java for the Dutch East India Company, started to map parts of the west coast and in 1616 Dirk Hartog set foot on his namesake island near Shark Bay. From this time on, Dutch, English and French navigators explored the west coast - Abel Tasman in 1644 and William Dampier in 1688 explored the Kimberley in some detail and recorded meetings with its Aboriginal people. Europeans did not attempt to settle the region until pastoralists in the 1880s came west looking for new grazing land. A gold rush at Halls Creek in 1885 brought 2000 prospectors to the town but most moved on within a couple of years when gold nuggets proved elusive. Many areas of the Kimberley were not settled until the 1920s – just a few generations ago – and transport and communication remained basic until the 1980s. The main highway between Fitzroy Crossing and Halls Creek wasn't sealed until 1986. Doubtless this isolation has served to protect much of the Kimberley's unique natural landscapes, wildlife and culture.

Left: Remote communities rely on the Royal Flying Doctor Service for regular health clinics and emergency help.

Far left: The bumpy Cape Leveque road preserves some of the benefits of isolation.

PEOPLE

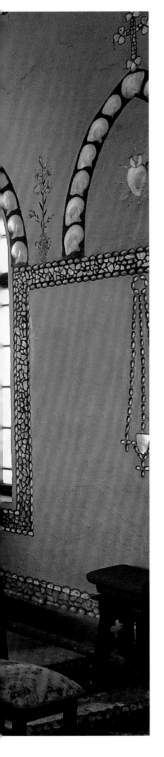

Not only is the geology of the Kimberley ancient but people have lived in this landscape for an incredibly long time. A fragment of the world's oldest known ground-edge axe was found at Carpenters Gap, a large rock shelter in Windjana Gorge National Park. The fragment of basalt had been polished by grinding it on a softer rock like sandstone until it was very smooth – around 45,000-49,000 years ago. Similarly, a Kimberley fragment of kangaroo bone worn as nose jewellery has been dated at 46,000 years old, making it Australia's oldest ornament. When pastoralists and gold miners arrived in the 1880s Aboriginal people began to be killed or pushed off their land. In the decades that followed many remained close to their country by working on cattle stations nearby but were forced into towns in the late 1960s – ironically when they won the right to fair wages but the work dried up. Losing their land was, and is, particularly painful as it is integral to their identity. Aboriginal people had no idea of owning the land in the sense that it was a possession that could be traded or given away, but saw themselves as custodians of land in which humans, animals and spirits were inseparable from the land – in fact, one and the same. Strange country was meaningless to them. To leave your country was to leave your world. Today almost half of the Kimberley's population is made up of Aboriginal people, belonging to more than 30 traditional language groups. Many live in small communities or towns close to their traditional lands but battle disadvantage in employment, education and health.

Above: Love of Aussie Rules football unites the Kimberley and many players go on to play for the national Australian Football League.

Left: Several missions were established in the Kimberley in the late nineteenth century to convert the local Aboriginal people. The Sacred Heart Church at Beagle Bay was built by German Pallottine missionaries in 1917 with this unique pearl shell altar.

ECONOMY

The Kimberley covers 424,517 kilometres, about the size of Sweden, yet is home to just 40,000 people and more than 40 per cent live in or around Broome. The pastoral industry was one of the earliest industries in the Kimberley and pastoral leases for grazing stock still cover about half of the region and bring the economy close to $200 million a year. Some of the cattle stations on the Gibb River Road supplement their income by providing accommodation or tours and this can be a wonderful opportunity to see some remote country and meet these hardy, resilient people. Mining is by far the greatest contributor to the economy, worth about 1 billion dollars, mostly from iron ore but also diamonds, crude oil, nickel, copper, cobalt, gold and silver. About 300,000 visitors come to the Kimberley each year, spending about $300 million, and are mostly domestic travellers rather than international. Other important industries are pearling and agriculture. The Ord River Irrigation Area made 14,000 hectares available for agriculture in the 1970s and another 13,400 hectares was made available in 2013, with plans for more to come. The area grows sugar cane and sandalwood, plus fruit, vegetable and seed crops.

Left: Land use has gradually changed from agriculture to forestry in these irrigated fields near Kununurra.

Below: Cattle muster at Louisa Downs. Kimberley cattle station life was immortalised by Dame Mary Durack in the Australian classic *Kings in Grass Castles*.

CULTURE

One of the most rewarding and interesting aspects of a visit to the Kimberley is encountering the living culture of its traditional Aboriginal owners, who make up almost half of the region's population. Every traveller will encounter the concept of the 'Dreaming'. This word attempts to explain a complex concept that lies at the heart of Aboriginal culture and should not be understood in the English context of something that is not real. It describes a creation period when ancestral beings shaped the landscape wherever they went yet the Dreaming is not part of the past, it lies within the present and will determine the future. Ancestral beings have a permanent presence in spiritual or physical form. This is the source of all knowledge, stories, ceremonies, landscapes, plants and animals, art and rules for living. Certain places where ancestral beings live are sacred and those sites, stories or ceremonies may only be viewed by certain people – initiated men only or perhaps just by women – and this is why some sites are off limits to visitors. Similarly, an artist may only paint his or her own stories and landscapes, and it may not be appropriate for the layers of meaning within the painting to be revealed to strangers. The Kimberley has a wealth of marvelous rock art sites with two very distinct styles, the ancient Gwion Gwion (Bradshaw) and more recent Wanjina.

Above: Art is still an expression of culture and country for local people such as artist Judy Mengil who sells her work through Kununurra's Waringarri Aboriginal Arts gallery.

Left: Gwion Gwion art, like these paintings on Jar Island, is predominantly populated by graceful, detailed and well-proportioned human figures, often elaborately adorned and accompanied by weapons such as spears, spearthrowers and boomerangs. Many of these art sites can only been seen on boat cruises that explore the coastline north of Broome.

Far left: Guide Sylvester Mangolamara (also pictured left) evokes the power of the electrifying sea spirit Kaiara and the smaller, white spirit beings of the Wanjina period. These paintings typically feature a white clay background overlaid with yellow and reddish-brown ochre figures sporting charcoal eyes.

WILDLIFE

Left: The beautiful rainbow bee eater keeps its eggs safe in a nesting chamber at the end of a tunnel that is almost a metre long.

Below: The planigale is one of many small marsupial species in the Kimberley. This tiny carnivorous marsupial 'mouse' has a pouch that opens backwards. Her young migrate here after birth and develop in the pouch for about 28 days.

Opposite page: The green tree frog is found in tree hollows and often in bathrooms. It wipes itself with a waxy secretion to minimize moisture loss during the day and tucks its limbs and chin in so less skin is exposed.

There is so much space in the Kimberley and so few people, not to mention plenty of water, that an incredible variety of wildlife thrives here. There are more than 300 species of birds, from the jabiru and brolga to parrots, kites, eagles, owls, honeyeaters and bowerbirds. Mammals such as kangaroos, wallabies, echidnas, bandicoots, bilbies and quolls can be hard to spot as many species are nocturnal or resting in a shady spot in the heat of the day so you will have most success at dawn and dusk. You're more likely to see reptiles such as the frill-necked lizard, goannas, geckos and water monitors. Of course, no reptile inspires more fascination and fear than the saltwater crocodile, found in the Kimberley's tidal rivers, mangrove shores, estuaries and billabongs. The freshwater crocodile is also common and although not considered dangerous, it's best not to approach them. The Kimberley coast too is a special place for wildlife. You can see enormous flocks of migratory shore-birds at the Broome Bird Observatory, cruise with humpback whales as they migrate north to calve (June to September) in the Lalang-garram/Camden Sound Marine Park, and watch Flatback turtles nesting by night (October to February). If you are lucky you may see the delightful Australian snubfin dolphin (*Orcaella heinsohni*) in Roebuck Bay and along the Dampier Peninsula coastline, recognised as a new species in 2005.

Left: The Gould's goanna is a common species of monitor lizard. They grow to an average length of 140 cm on a diet of insects, mice, snakes, birds and other lizards.

Right: The saltwater or estuarine crocodile can grow up to 6 m long and is a fierce predator. Despite the name, they can be found a long way upstream. Observe the warning signs and check with locals but if you are in any doubt whether it's safe to swim, don't risk it. The harmless freshwater crocodile, like this one at Geikie Gorge (bottom right), can be distinguished by its narrow snout, tapering to a point at the end.

Below left: Fiddler crab in the mangrove mudflats near Wyndham.

Far left: A rare spiny-tailed gecko sloughing off its skin on some dried spinifex at El Questro.

PLANTLIFE

This vast and diverse landscape has thousands of fascinating plant species, many of them rare or unique to the Kimberley, such as the boab, and botanists suspect there are still many new species to be found in its remote gorges and coastlines. The tropical savannah that surrounds the region's range country is common in other parts of the world yet the Kimberley's savannah is considered an outstanding example of this type of landscape because it has been so little modified. The most common trees in this grassy woodland are boabs and bloodwood, plus stringybark and woollybutt eucalypts in wetter areas. In the sheltered gorges of the north, where the most rain falls, there are patches of rare monsoon forests, livistona palms and cycads. The stunted pindan woodland of the Dampier Peninsula is dominated by wattles, the region's watercourses are lined with paperbarks, pandanus and water lilies, and its coastal estuaries are fringed with mangroves. Life in the tropics is a tale of two worlds for the plants of the Kimberley. The land is lush, green and bursting with life in the Wet yet very hot and dry for many months of the year. Some of the region's most distinctive plants have adapted to this environment by losing their leaves in the dry season to reduce moisture loss – the boab, kapok bush and Kimberley rose.

Above: Open savannah woodland near Windjana gorge.

Right: The Kimberley Rose, or Sticky Kurrajong, is a deciduous tree that sheds its leaves early in the dry season and blooms from April to December.

Far right: Tropical water lily. A new species of water lily, blue peony, was identified in an area off the Gibb River Road in 2015.

Left: Velvety fruit from the boab is rich in protein and vitamin C. In Australia the boab is found only in the Kimberley and a neighbouring area of the NT and may live for more than 1000 years.

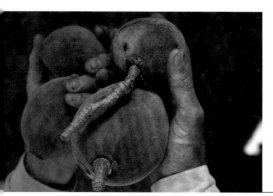

Above: The roots of the common rock fig can penetrate 500 m into rock crevices to find water.

Left: The yellow kapok shrub's buttercup-like flowers form large pods encasing seeds surrounded by a fluffy down. It's not the same species of kapok used for stuffing pillows but the down has been used for ceremonial body decoration.

KUNUNURRA

Surrounded by range country and the bountiful waters of the Ord River, Kununurra has perhaps the most picturesque setting of any Kimberley town. Built in the 1960s as a service town for the Ord River Irrigation Scheme, the town has matured into a confident and growing community supported by agriculture, diamond mining and tourism. The river is damned to the south of Kununurra, forming Lake Argyle, Australia's largest inland waterway, and holding back the wet season water so the Ord can flow steadily all year around. The lake and river lie beneath the Carr Boyd Ranges, typically rugged Kimberley sandstone, and are strikingly beautiful. A boat or canoe trip from Lake Argyle to Kununurra along the upper Ord River, through 55 km of ranges, gorges and lush greenery, is one of the region's highlights. Comfortable accommodation, services and a wide range of tours make Kununurra an ideal base for exploring the east Kimberley.

Above: On Kununurra's eastern border, Mirima National Park is a pocket of red sandstone outcrops, with similarities to the Bungle Bungle range. There are two short walks in Hidden Valley, an oasis of beehive domes and ridges among boabs and ghost gums. The lookout in the park is a fine spot to watch sunset or sunrise, as is Kelly's Knob, the steep-sided hill just north of town.

Left: The biggest pink rough diamond ever discovered in Australia, this 12.76 carat Argyle Pink Jubilee Diamond, came from the Arygle Diamond Mine, one of the largest diamond producers in the world. Owned by Rio Tinto Group on land leased from its traditional owners, Argyle is known for its coloured diamonds – cognac and champagne, plus rare pink, red, and violet. Since 1983 the mine has produced more than 800 million rough carats but it is set to close in 2021.

LAKE ARGYLE

Every wet season the Ord River used to carry a huge volume of water from the Durack Range to the Cambridge Gulf but there was hardly any flow during the dry season. In the 1940s and 50s pastoralists and state government experimented with different crops and decided to dam the river to create a water supply for the fertile river flats downstream. The Diversion Dam, built on Kununurra's western border in 1963, raises the river level so that the sugar cane and fruit crops growing on the Ivanhoe plain can be irrigated without pumping. Below the dam, the Lower Ord flows out to Cambridge Gulf, and despite damning and irrigation 80 per cent of the Ord's flow still reaches the sea. Saltwater crocodiles are found only in this lower part of the river as they can't get above the dam to the waters called Lake Kununurra. This lake and its many lagoons are a lush series of waterways, full of birds, fish and freshwater crocodiles. If you follow the river upstream from here for 55 km you'll reach Lake Argyle and the Ord River Dam but by road the lake is 70 km south of town. The Argyle Diamond Mine is just south of the lake and can be visited by an aerial tour from Kununurra.

Previous page: The tranquil waters of Lake Argyle are perfect for canoeing, a wonderful way to see wildlife and explore at your own pace. Several operators supply transport, equipment and permanent camps for multi-day self-guided trips down the Ord River, leaving from Lake Argyle. If you don't have the muscle for that option, speedboat trips are also excellent.

■ Lake Argyle is a freshwater reservoir with a capacity 21 times that of Sydney Harbour. There are more than 70 islands in the lake - the tips of hills submerged when the Ord River Dam was built. Now it's home to an estimated 35,000 freshwater crocodiles, a colony of short eared rock wallabies and more than 270 species of birds, including the elegant jabiru, or black necked stork, below.

HIGHWAY 1

The Gibb River Road is one of Australia's great outback drives but if time or resources compel you to take the sealed Great Northern Highway route from Kununurra to Broome (1043 km) this is not necessarily the second-best option. The stretch between Kununurra and Halls Creek is one of the most scenic bits of highway in the country, and it also gives you a chance to see the magnificent Purnululu National Park and visit The Warmun Arts Centre. In this creative community's gallery you can see the minimal and elegant artworks of the Gija people in the style made famous by Rover Thomas, Queenie McKenzie and Lena Nyadbi. Just past Halls Creek is the junction to the unsealed Tanami Track which leads south to the 300,000-year-old Wolfe Creek Meteor Crater (145 km). Back on the main highway, further west, near Fitzroy Crossing you can take a boat down Geike Gorge to see its 30 metre walls of ancient limestone barrier reef. For a big Kimberley adventure, take both of these roads to drive a loop back to your starting point.

Left: The cliffs of Geikie Gorge, named Danggu by the Bunuba traditional owners, are studded with fossils and caves. Wet season flooding scours the lower walls to create the striking line of clean white sandstone. You're likely to see freshwater crocodiles and plenty of birdlife on a boat cruise.

Below: The Warmun art movement is distinctive for its simple forms, subtle colours from natural ochre pigment and canvases grainy with coloured earth or black ash. The Warmun Arts Centre gallery is generally open 9-4 on weekdays but call ahead for permission to enter the community.

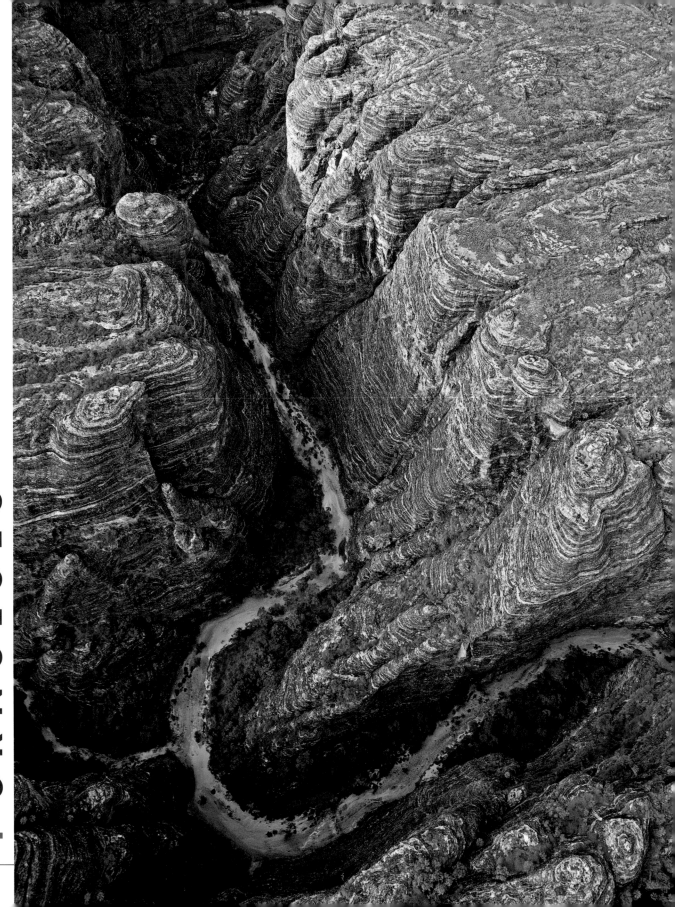

Above: Pebbles worn smooth by seasonal floodwaters in Piccaninny Gorge. Most trails involve walking on pebbles or over boulders so make sure you have sturdy footwear.

Left: Scenic flights are available from Bellburn airstrip inside the park, or from Kununurra, and offer incredible perspectives of the domes.

Previous page: Cathedral Gorge (3 km return) is known for its wonderful acoustics. The pool shrinks as the season goes on.

One of Australia's most remote and magnificent national parks, Purnululu National Park was listed as a World Heritage Site in 2003, yet few Australians had even heard of it. In fact, until the 1980s Purnululu was known only to its Jaru and Gija custodians and a few cattle drovers. When a documentary crew filmed aerial footage in 1983 the secret was out and the distinctive sandstone 'beehive' domes of the Bungle Bungle range became protected by national park status in 1987. The domes are found in the southern area of the park where the Piccaninny Creek bed winds through this surreal landscape of rippled rock, unlike any other in Australia. The western part of the range is a long imposing wall of conglomerate rock up to 200 m high, eroded into deep narrow chasms lined with majestic Livistona fan palms. The access road is a rough 50 km 4WD track that keeps the number of ground visitors low – around 30,000 per year (compared to Uluru's 300,000) – but this park has an otherworldly beauty well worth the effort to get there. Especially if you can stay a few nights. There are scenic flights from Kununurra and nearby resorts, and plenty of guided tour options for those not equipped to self-drive.

PURNULULU

The Bungle Bungle Range is composed of Devonian-age quartz sandstone. The beehive-shaped towers were created as water eroded the range over the past 20 million years. Their distinctive stripes are a fragile cyanobacterial crust just a few millimetres thin. The layers are grey where clay particles hold remnants of the wet season's deluge for long enough to encourage cyanobacteria to live and orange where iron oxide has leached to the surface. Cyanobacteria are single-celled organisms that represent some of the oldest life forms on earth. Purnululu's ancient and fragile sandstone towers are considered the most outstanding example of cone karst in sandstones anywhere in the world and it was this unique geology, plus its 'exceptional natural beauty', that won the park its World Heritage listing.

Above: The Picaninny Gorge Trail (30 km return) is a long trail for experienced walkers but one of best walks in the park is to start this trail, following the dry bed of Picaninny Creek until you've had enough and return, for this provides spectacular perspectives on the domes the whole way (14 km return to the 'elbow'). Walkers going the whole distance must register with the Visitors Centre.

Left: Golden rays ignite Mini Palms Gorge (5 km return), a cool refuge. Livistona palms thrive in clefts and gorges of the 33 km long by 23 km wide Bungle Bungle Range.

Following page: Brancos Lookout, El Questro.

EL QUESTRO

Above: A mating pair of brolgas, one of more than 100 bird species in the park, including Rainbow bee eaters and the rare Gouldian Finch.

Left: The waterfall in Emma Gorge, one of the most beautiful in the Kimberley, is a reached via a challenging 3 km (2 hours) return walk.

This vast privately-owned tract of wilderness is a working cattle station with a herd of about 6000 head. Fortunately, this spectacular country is also open to tourists with three resorts offering a range of accommodation from camping and cabins to the luxurious Homestead. At a million acres, that's 80 kilometres long by 60 kilometres wide, there is much to explore. El Questro's treasure is its abundant water – the wilderness park offers countless gorges, swimming holes, waterfalls and natural springs, as well as ancient rock art and a wealth of flora and fauna. Of many excellent adventurous walks, one of the most exciting is the El Questro Gorge walk, leading up a narrow gorge with towering fern-covered walls, rock pools and lots of boulder hopping (7 km, 4-5 hours). The Chamberlain Gorge cruise is one of the most popular activities, a peaceful way to see El Questro's abundant wildlife and waterholes, but if your budget can stretch to the Explosion Gorge cruise, it's a more intimate and dramatic trip. The resorts offer many other guided tours plus fishing, horseriding and scenic flights. The track off the Gibb River Rd is unsealed for 16 km so a 4WD is required for the Station but not for Emma Gorge.

GIBB RIVER ROAD

Gibb River Road leads from Derby to Kununurra and passes through remote range country and grass plains, threaded with creeks, gorges, swimming holes and waterfalls. It also provides access to the northern Kimberley along the more rugged Kalumbaru Road to the Mitchell Plateau. This legendary road is both an experience and a challenge - 660 km of mostly unsealed gravel and dirt, created in the 1960s as a way for the cattle stations of this region to get their stock to Derby and Wyndham ports. Although now used more frequently by travellers, the alarming sight of a huge cattle road train barrelling along in clouds of dust is still common. Part of the Gibb River Road experience is staying at the cattle stations along the way, meeting their owners and perhaps taking a scenic flight or tour to explore privately owned landscapes seen by few, such as Mt Elizabeth Station's rock art sites. There are also plenty of good campsites close to several beautiful gorges where you can go for a walk or swim.

Previous page: Rising 300 metres above the Lennard River, Windjana Gorge slices through the ancient limestone reef of the Napier Range, part of a great inland sea that covered the Kimberley 350 million years ago. From a cave located 40 metres above the river's present level, geologists have unearthed the fossilised bones of an extinct seven metre-long crocodile and ancient turtles.

There are so many beautiful gorges in this area and it would take weeks to explore them all. Bell Gorge (left) is considered the fairest of all and so gets the most attention but there are plenty of quiet gems like Adcock Gorge (above).

Left: Pentecost river crossing with the Cockburn Range in the background.
Do not be tempted to walk in to check the depth - saltwater crocodiles are found here.

Above: The view from Mt Leake at the Mornington Wildlife Sanctuary - owned and managed by the not-for-profit organisation Australian Wilderness Conservancy. Protecting 3000 square kilometres of stunning gorges and abundant wildlife, their Wilderness Camp is a fascinating place to stay as the focus is on conservation work.

Right: Mornington Wildlife Sanctuary protects one of the last remaining populations of the Gouldian Finch, once found in the millions in Northern Australia and now reduced to about 2500.

The Gibb River Road is generally open from April to October and road conditions have been much improved in the last few years. Bitumen has been laid over steep hill sections and nearly all the creek and river crossings now have concrete bottoms. Although not as rough as it used to be, it can be badly corrugated and you need to plan your fuel stops carefully. It's generally a 4WD route because of the need for high clearance in places. In the middle of the season when rivers are low it may be possible to use a 2WD but you'll need to check road conditions and you won't be able to access some side tracks. This is a very busy route in high season but it's still a remote wilderness area and your vehicle needs to be in good condition and equipped with extra fuel, water and spare wheels.

MITCHELL PLATEAU

The Mitchell Plateau encompasses some of the most wild, remote and sparsely populated country in Australia. It also has some of the most spectacular scenery, waterfalls and rock art in the country so it's well worth the considerable effort it takes to get here. Mitchell River National Park was gazetted in 2000 and protects the beautiful Punamii-unpuu, the Mitchell Falls, an area of great cultural significance to the Wunambal people and home to the ancestor rainbow serpent, Wunggurr. Walking to the falls through the park's patches of rainforest, groves of Livistona fan palms, grey box woodland and creeks lined with pandanus and paperbarks may be one of the best things you do in the Kimberley. From the Mitchell Falls campsite to the edge of the falls will take you about 2.5 hours. At Little Mertens Falls you can swim in rock pools and explore a cave behind the waterfall where there are some Gwion Gwion rock paintings. The next stop is Big Mertens Falls, a 60 m waterfall, before you reach the four-tier Mitchell Falls. It's possible to take a helicopter from the falls back to the campsite and this gives you the best of both worlds.

■ Above: The Mertens Water Monitor found in this park has nostrils on the top of its head which allows it to remain partially submerged like a crocodile when looking for its prey – fish, frogs and insects.

■ To see Little Mertens Falls you'll need to take the 4WD-only Kalumbaru Road north for 60 km from the Gibb River Road to Drysdale River Station, your last stop for fuel, provisions or a drink at the bar, then continue for another 100 km to the Mitchell Plateau Track. From here its 85 km to the Mitchell Falls camping area and the start of the walking track. You'll need a permit to traverse this region, called the Ngauwudu Road Zone pass.

Previous page: Mitchell Falls.

DERBY

Derby sits on a narrow spur of land surrounded by tidal mud flats, close to where the mighty Fitzroy River flows into King Sound. The entrance to the sound is a maze of a thousand islands, the Buccaneer Archipelago, a spectacular area to explore by boat or plane. Very little of it is accessible by land because the terrain is just so remote and rugged that there are simply no roads into the coastal regions. The town was one of the earliest in the Kimberley, established in 1883 as a port for wool and pearl shell exports, and the port is still used for fishing, tourism and mining operations. The unusual D-shaped jetty has been constructed to cope with the highest tide in Australia (11.8 m) and is a popular place to watch the sun set. The small town has a population of 3500 but is the Kimberley's third largest. Derby's position at the start of the Gibb River Road and close to the Kimberley coast makes it a good place to pick up supplies, and scenic flights and cruises can be more economical here than options in Broome or Wyndham.

Above: Boab trees are common in the landscape and streets of Derby. The town's so-called 'Prison Tree' is thought to be about 1500 years old and its girth is almost 15 m but there is no evidence it was ever used as a lock-up. Instead it is thought to have been used by indigenous people for storing bones and is now fenced off as a sacred site.

Right: The Horizontal Waterfall at Talbot Bay in the Buccaneer Archipelago. Huge tidal movements force seawater through a narrow gap, creating waves and whirlpools that churn like a waterfall.

DAMPIER PENINSULA

Forming a large triangle north of Broome, the Dampier Peninsula is a wild and beautiful expanse of Pindan country, cliffs, beaches, crystal clear water, mangroves and salt plains. It's home to Aboriginal people of six different language groups, the Ngumbarl, Jabirr Jabirr, Nyul Nyul, Nimanburu, Bardi Jawi and Goolarabooloo peoples, who call the peninsula Ardi, simply meaning north. Many of these small Indigenous communities offer a chance to understand their culture and environment with accommodation options and rewarding tours – you might catch mud crabs, learn to make a spear, try bush foods or go walking. On the edge of Roebuck Bay, the Broome Bird Observatory is one of the best places in Australia to see migratory seabirds. At Willie Creek and Cygnet Bay you can learn about pearl farming, and at the Beagle Bay community you can visit the pearl shell altar in their extraordinary Sacred Heart Church (see page 10), a little further north there's a humpback whale nursery at Pender Bay and a trochus hatchery at the tip of the peninsula at One Arm Point.

■ Barred Creek, 40 km north of Broome, is a good camping, mudcrabbing and fishing spot.

Above: Distinctive red Pindan cliffs north of James Price Point. Just one rough mostly unsealed road traverses the peninsula, the 220 km Cape Leveque road. It's 4WD only but tours and car hire are available from Broome.

Below: On the Lurujarri Heritage Trail, Goolarabooloo lawman Richard Hunter shows the feather fossil of Marella – from the emu man creation story. Modern science tells us these are fossilized cycads. This nine day (82 km) walk follows the traditional Song Cycle of the Goolarabooloo people. The community runs this very special guided walk several times a year during the dry season.

B R O O M E

ITurquoise water, red cliffs, white sand and green mangroves – Broome is a town full of vivid colour and tropical lushness, together with an interesting history and a composition quite unlike any other Australian town. It was established on the shore of Roebuck Bay in the 1890s as a telegraph cable station and a base for pearl shell merchants and their divers. The first pearl divers were Aboriginal, then later Malaysian, Indonesian, Filipino, Chinese or Japanese. Consequently the people of Broome are an unusual mix of Aboriginal, Asian and European heritage. When plastic buttons were invented in the 1950s the market for pearl shell crashed but Broome survived by learning to produce cultured pearls and has since prospered, not only on the profits from the world's biggest and most lustrous pearls, but also from ever-booming tourism. Refined and expensive resorts at Cable Beach have brought the town much attention and sophistication, and although it is probably true that Broome has lost some of its unique character, it remains a fascinating oasis and very enjoyable place to spend a few days.

Above: Classic Broome colours at Roebuck Bay.

Right: This 22 km-long flat stretch of white sand is named after the international telegraph cable that came ashore here in 1889 from Java, which in turn was linked to London. In peak season it's busy with cars, camel rides (left) and visitors toasting the sunset but if you just keep walking, or driving, you'll have it all to yourself. Be sure to check the tide times as the difference between high and low tide can be as much as 10 metres.

Previous page: Sun Cinemas, the world's oldest outdoor cinema (opened in 1916), where deck chairs await in rows under the night sky.

BROOME

Before the Japanese developed techniques for growing cultured pearls, finding a pearl was a rare piece of good fortune. Only one oyster in thousands has a pearl and even at the beginning of last century they were worth many thousands of pounds. The main trade was in pearl shell – used for mother-of-pearl buttons, cutlery handles and ornaments. It was a lucrative but dangerous industry with a very high mortality rate. In the early days skin divers descended up to 18 m without equipment but by the 1880s divers were wearing heavy brass helmets and suits with an air hose. Decompression sickness (nitrogen bubbles in body tissues) was not understood and many divers died or were disabled by 'the bends' until 1918 when Broome divers began to follow Navy diving tables that mandated staged ascents. At peak in the early 1900s, the town's 400 pearl luggers (boats) supplied 80 per cent of the world's mother of pearl. The pearl industry is still a lucrative one, worth about 70 million dollars to the Kimberley's economy, but the oysters are now carefully cosseted in pearl farms. It takes about 2 years after insertion of a 'nucleus' into the flesh of the Pinctada Maxima oyster for layers of nacre to form around the irritant and become an Australian South Sea Pearl.

■ The town's Japanese cemetery is the resting place of 919 Japanese divers who lost their lives working in the industry.

Top left: Cultured pearls are grown in oysters suspended in nets in the warm Kimberley waters. To learn more you can visit a pearl farm at Willie Creek or Cygnet Bay.

Left: Cultured pearls are graded by size. You can explore original pearl luggers on Dampier Terrace, as well as jewellery shops, such as Paspaley or Kailis, selling world class pearls.

ACKNOWLEDGEMENTS

The author would like to thank all the talented photographers whose work is included here. She would particularly like to thank Simon Nevill, Craig Lewis and Cec Richardson. Katrina would also like to thank Andrew Swaffer for his enthusiasm and commissioning the series; Christine Schiedel for her skill and patience; and Jo Runciman, Lauren Smith, Jess Teideman and Rebecca Cotton at Australian Geographic for their help. Thanks to Tourism Australia, Lana Mitchell at RFDS and Samantha McLean at Parks Australia. And finally, love and thanks always to Charlie Burrows.

ABOUT THE AUTHOR

Katrina O'Brien is the author of Australia's bestselling walking guide, *Sydney's Best Harbour* & *Coastal Walks*. She first fell in love with the Red Centre and the Kimberley while travelling and writing her way around Australia for two years as the co-author of the travel guides *Footprint Australia Handbook* and *Footprint West Coast Handbook*. When not researching and writing walking and travel guides Katrina is a book publishing consultant and has previously worked as Managing Editor for Murdoch Books and Penguin Lantern.

ABOUT THE PUBLISHERS

The Australian Geographic journal is a geographical magazine founded by Dick Smith in 1986. It mainly covers stories about Australia - its geography, culture, wildlife and people - and six editions are published every year. Australian Geographic also publish a number of books every year on similar subjects for both children and adults. A portion of the profits goes to the Australian Geographic Society which supports scientific research as well as environmental conservation, community projects and Australian adventurers.

Woodslane Press are a book publishing company based in Sydney, Australia. They are the publishers of Australia's best-selling walking guides and under their co-owned Boiling Billy imprint also publish camping, bush exploration and 4WD guides. For more than a decade committed to publishing books that empower Australians to better explore and understand their own country, Woodslane Press is proud to be working with Australian Geographic to produce this new series of souvenir books.

Also available:

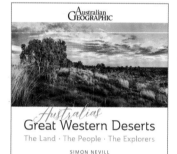